HOW DO BATS SEE IN THE DARK?

Questions and Answers About Night Creatures

BY MELVIN AND GILDA BERGER

ILLUSTRATED BY JIM EFFLER

CONTENTS

KEY TO ABBREVIATIONS

cm = centimeter/centimetre
g = gram
km = kilometer/kilometre
kph = kilometers/kilometres per hour
m = meter/metre

Text copyright © 2000 by Melvin and Gilda Berger
Illustrations copyright © 2000 by Jim Effler
All rights reserved. Published by Scholastic Inc.
SCHOLASTIC and associated logos are trademarks and/or registered trademarks of Scholastic Inc.

No part of this publication may be reproduced, or stored in a retrieval system, or transmitted in any form or by any means, electronic, mechanical, photocopying, recording, or otherwise, without written permission of the publisher. For information regarding permission, write to Scholastic Inc., Attention: Permissions Department, 555 Broadway, New York, NY 10012.

Library of Congress Cataloging-in-Publication Data

Berger, Melvin.
    How do bats see in the dark?: questions and answers about night creatures / by Melvin and Gilda Berger; illustrated by Jim Effler.
    p.   cm. — (Scholastic question and answer series)
    Includes index.
    Summary: Questions and answers present the habitats and behavior of a variety of nocturnal animals, from cats and kiwis to bats, owls, and foxes.
    1. Nocturnal animals—Miscellanea—Juvenile literature. [1. Nocturnal animals—Miscellanea. 2. Questions and answers.] I. Berger, Gilda. II. Effler, James M., 1956– ill. III. Title.
QL755.5 .B57 2000   591.5'18–dc21   00-023930
ISBN 0-439-22904-9

Book design by David Saylor and Nancy Sabato

10 9 8 7   04

Printed in the U.S.A.   08
First trade printing, October 2001

Expert Readers:
Don Moore, Curator of Animals
Anthony Brownie, Supervisor, Animal Department
Central Park Wildlife Center, New York, NY

For Mitch, our favorite night person
— M. AND G. BERGER

To Herbert and JoAnne, who get up long
before these animals call it a night
— J. EFFLER

INTRODUCTION

Did you know that many animals—bats and owls, raccoons and skunks, lions and leopards, fireflies and cockroaches—wake up around the time you go to sleep?

These night creatures, or nocturnal animals, mostly rest or sleep during the day. But when it's dark, they get busy, usually looking for food.

Very few animals are active only by night or only by day. All night creatures, though, are much more active after dark than they are when the sun is shining brightly.

Night creatures are well suited for the life they lead. They have very sharp senses to help them find their way in darkness. A few have special senses to help them "see" at night by listening for echoes or feeling other animals' body heat. Many are black or gray in color to help them hide and avoid enemies.

Animals prefer nighttime for many reasons. Their daytime enemies can't find them. They can feed on animals or plants that only come out or open in the dark. They don't have to compete with daytime animals for the same food. And they avoid the heat and drying effects of the sun.

How do scientists learn about nocturnal animals? They go out at night and look and listen carefully to what they see and hear. You'll be amazed at what they've discovered about animals that are wide awake when you're fast asleep!

Melvin Berger   Gilda Berger

IN THE AIR

How do bats see in the dark?

With their ears! As they fly, most bats make a series of very high-pitched squeaks, or clicks, that are usually too high for us to hear. The clicks strike and bounce off nearby objects and are heard by the bat when the echo returns.

A sound that echoes back quickly lets bats know an object is close. A sound that takes longer to return means the object is farther away. Using sound to find things is called echolocation. Echolocation lets bats see in the dark!

What do most bats eat?

Insects that fly at night. A single brown bat can catch up to 600 insects in an hour!

What do bats eat besides insects?

Fruit, nectar, and pollen from plants; frogs, fish, birds, and other animals; or even blood. There are nearly 1,000 different kinds of bats. Each kind is suited for the life it leads. By looking closely at a bat, you can usually guess what it eats.

Bats that eat insects, for example, have especially large ears to pick up echoes. Plant-eating bats have long tongues to reach deep into night-blooming flowers and lap up the nectar. Vampire bats have special heat-sensing organs to find the blood vessels on their prey. Fishing bats have sharp, hooklike claws to grab slippery fish. And meat eaters have sharp teeth to feed on other bats, rodents, and frogs.

Why do bats fly at night?

A few reasons. Insect-eating bats feast on moths and mosquitoes that come out at night. Plant eaters feed on the nectar of plants that open only after dark. And night is the best time for vampire bats to find the sleeping animals they seek.

Daytime birds also eat insects. Daytime butterflies also suck nectar. By flying at night, bats don't have to compete with these animals for their food.

Lesser long-nosed bat

Little brown bats

Do vampire bats attack humans?

Very rarely. Their usual prey are sleeping cattle or horses.

At night, a vampire bat hovers in the air like a hummingbird, emitting squeaks. When its echoes indicate a large animal that's not moving, the vampire bat swoops down. Walking silently, the bat sneaks up on the victim and makes a tiny cut with its sharp teeth. As the blood oozes out, the bat laps up 1 to 2 ounces (28 to 57 g)—a full day's supply. Then away it flies, often before the victim even wakes up.

Are bats bad?

Not at all. In fact, bats help us. Insect-eating bats gulp down huge numbers of insect pests. Fruit-eating bats help spread seeds and pollinate plants. And the manure, or guano, that bats produce is a valuable fertilizer.

Some people think bats are mean because of their strange features, such as giant ears or large nose flaps. But these features are important. Big ears help bats with echolocation. The nose flap lets them direct the sounds they make. Far from mean, bats are gentle and intelligent creatures of the night.

How do bats sleep?

Upside down. When bats settle down for a long day's rest, they fold their wings around themselves and hang upside down in a cave or other dark place. Usually, many bats rest together. Large fruit bats often hang from branches, like pieces of fruit. Other bats dangle from ledges or tree trunks.

Female bats even give birth while hanging upside down. Usually just one baby bat is born at a time.

Are bats birds?

No. Bats are warm-blooded mammals, just like cats and dogs, lions and tigers, and humans. Like most other mammals, bats grow inside their mothers and are born alive. When they're very young, the babies get milk from their mother's body. When grown, they have hair or fur on their skin. No bird fits that description!

But bats are different from all other mammals. They can fly. The skin of their wings, which is stretched over their long fingers, is thinner than a plastic bag!

Which insects often escape bats?

Certain moths. Noctuid (NOK-too-id) moths can hear the high-pitched bat squeaks. As a bat comes close, these moths loop and spiral through the air. This confuses the bat and helps the moths escape.

Arctiid (ARK-tih-id) moths make sounds and clicks that a bat can hear. This disturbs the bat's echolocation, making it hard for the bat to catch them.

Other insects, like lacewings, just fold their wings and drop straight down to the ground when bats are too close. There the lacewings are safe—at least for a while.

Why do moths fly around a light?

They may mistake the light for the moon. Moths navigate by the moon. When they see a lightbulb, they get confused and fly toward it. No doubt you've seen a moth fly around and around a bulb. If the moth gets too near, the heat of the bulb burns its wings, and it dies.

Which moth looks like a hummingbird?

The sphinx moth. This large nighttime moth flies toward flowers that are light-colored or strongly scented. Beating its wings about 35 times a second, the sphinx moth flutters over the flowers like a small hummingbird.

The sphinx moth uncoils its long, tubelike mouth, called a proboscis (pro-BOS-iss), and reaches inside to suck the nectar. In some sphinx moths, the proboscis measures 11 inches (28 cm), which is longer than the moth's entire body!

How do moths find their mates?

By smell. Female luna moths give off a powerful odor into the night air. Male luna moths pick up the smell with their feathery antennae, or feelers. Guided by their sense of smell, the males can find females more than 5 miles (8 km) away!

White-lined sphinx moths

Snowy owl

Are most birds night flyers?

No. Almost all birds are diurnal, that is, active only during the day. Just owls, whippoorwills, and a few other kinds of birds search for food at night.

Can owls see well?

Yes. Owls have gigantic eyes. The central pupil, or dark part of the eye, is extra-large to let in maximum light. This helps the owl see—and catch—small animals in nearly total darkness. Owls see about 10 times better at night than you do.

What makes owls' eyes shine in the dark?

A layer of cells behind the eye, called the tapetum (tuh-PEE-tum). The tapetum works like a mirror. It reflects back any light that enters the eye. The tapetum helps the owl see in very dim light.

Do owls depend more on sight or hearing?

Hearing. The owl's very sensitive ears can pick up the softest sounds. In fact, experts say that a flying owl can hear a sound as faint as a mouse chewing grass under the snow!

In owls, one ear is lower and different in size and shape than the other. This makes the owl very good at finding the exact source of a sound. Also, the owl's face feathers form a disk that reflects sounds to the owl's large ear openings. No wonder owls are such good hunters!

Are owls truly wise?

Not really. Their large eyes make owls look very smart. But experts believe they are not as bright as many other birds. Some say that the owl's big eyes just don't leave enough room for a big brain!

Great horned owl

How do owls hunt?

They look and listen for prey in the dark. When an owl picks up a sound or smell, it silently swoops down toward its target. The owl's soft, fluffy-edged feathers muffle the sounds of its wings.

With sharp, hooked claws extended, the owl pounces on the victim and carries it away. Large owls nab rabbits, squirrels, and skunks. Smaller owls go after insects, mice, and other small animals.

Do owls chew their food?

No. Owls swallow small prey whole. But they rip larger prey into pieces before swallowing. Later, the owls cough up pellets of bone, fur, and feathers that they can't digest.

You may find pellets on the ground under an owl's nest or perch. A pile of pellets found recently contained the remains of about 2,000 mice, 210 rats, 92 blackbirds, and 4 frogs!

Where do owls sleep?

In thick plants and bushes, hollow trees, caves, or old buildings. The owls' dull colors and spotted feathers hide them from their enemies. Despite their name, barn owls also sleep in hollow trees or the rafters of abandoned buildings.

Do all owls "hoot"?

No, the only real hooter is the great horned owl. Other kinds of owls make different noises, from the barred owl's loud barks, to the long-eared owl's whining, catlike cry, to the barn owl's strange-sounding hiss.

In the country, you may hear a shrill whistly sound, running up and down the scale. Some superstitious people don't like this sound. They believe it signals a person's death. But you'll know it's only the cry of a screech owl in the dark.

Striped skunk

Whippoorwills

What bird cries its name all night long?

The male whippoorwill. While perched in a tree, this ghostly night flier sings out its name, "whippoorwill," about 16,000 times between sunset and sunrise! Curiously enough, whippoorwills only call when they are on a perch. They are silent when they fly.

People trying to fall asleep at night may get annoyed at the whippoorwill's cries. But farmers never complain. They're happy to have birds catching the insects that eat their growing crops.

People often call whippoorwills "nightjars" or "goatsuckers." The name nightjar is for the loud, repeated calls that jar people awake. And goatsucker comes from the old and incorrect belief that these night birds suck milk from female goats!

How do whippoorwills catch insects?

By flying with their mouths wide open. Also, around their mouths, the whippoorwills have long, curved facial whiskers that help scoop up bugs in the air.

Where are whippoorwills during the day?

Usually hiding on the forest floor. The whippoorwills' spotted brown feathers blend in with the leaves on the ground. Their excellent camouflage lets them rest safely on the ground from dawn to dusk without being seen.

Which night bird can't fly?

The kiwi of New Zealand. This bird has useless wings. It has neither good hearing nor good sight to help it hunt. But nostrils at the tip of a very long, flexible beak give the kiwi the best sense of smell of all birds. By poking and sniffing in the thick, wet forest floor, the kiwi finds earthworms, insects, and berries to eat. The little hairs around its beak may look strange, but they help the kiwi feel its way in the dark.

Are fireflies a kind of fly?

No. Fireflies, or lightning bugs, are small beetles. They fly together after sunset, each one producing a flashing light in its body. The fireflies make the light with certain chemicals in their bodies that mix together. Nothing burns to make the glow, so there's no heat.

On a summer night, you can see the fireflies' yellow lights flickering over fields and lawns. By day, the fireflies are well hidden in grass or weeds, or hanging motionless on the underside of leaves.

Some people collect fireflies in glass jars. But the light the bugs produce is very dim. So don't count on a jar filled with fireflies to light your way!

Why do fireflies glow?

To attract mates or prey. Each kind of firefly flashes its light off and on in a particular pattern. Since most female fireflies can't fly, they usually perch on the ground or in the bushes and wait. Sooner or later, a male hovers in the air around the female, flashing his special light signal. If the signal is right, the female flashes back—and the male flies over.

Does the firefly's glow also invite enemies?

No. Most firefly enemies, such as birds, frogs, lizards, and spiders, have learned that fireflies are best left alone. Fireflies contain a poison that can kill them.

What are glowworms?

The glowing larvae (LAR-vee) of some fireflies and their close relatives. In time, most glowworms, which look like tiny worms, develop into adult female fireflies.

One kind of glowworm lives in caves. Thousands of them group together. The light they make is bright enough to read by!

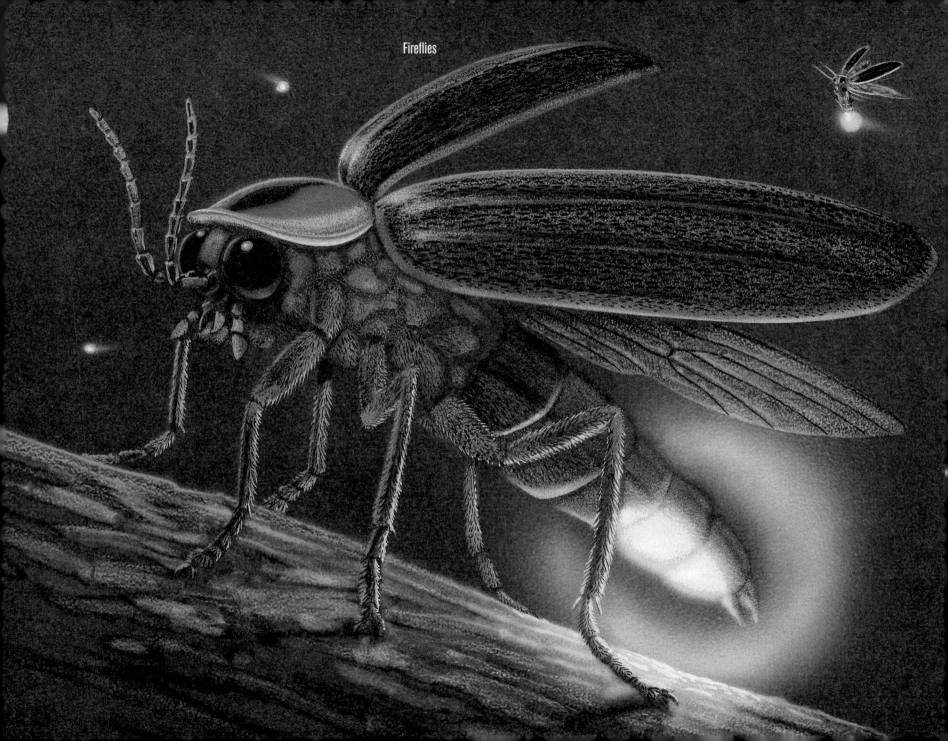

Flying squirrels

Do nighttime flying squirrels really fly?

No, they glide. Flying squirrels have extra flaps of
skin along the sides of their bodies. As the squirrel leaps
from a branch, it spreads out its limbs. Wings form, letting the squirrel
glide through the air.

The squirrel uses its bushy tail as a rudder to steer and keep its
balance. Flying squirrels can reach speeds of about 10 miles an hour
(16 kph) in the air.

Why do flying squirrels glide?

To keep safe. By gliding at night from tree to tree, the squirrels stay clear of enemies on the ground, such as snakes and weasels. Flying squirrels also escape attack by keen-sighted birds of prey, which usually hunt in the daytime.

But being active at night has its own dangers. Many a squirrel misses a branch or crashes into a tree it doesn't see. And night-feeding owls can easily nab flying squirrels in mid-flight.

Where are flying squirrels when it's light outside?

Asleep in hollow trees or abandoned woodpecker holes. The flying squirrels rest in nests lined with dry leaves, feathers or fur, and shredded bark.

Some flying squirrels live in the forests of Asia, Europe, and North America where winters can get very cold. These squirrels sleep rolled into a ball, heads covered with their heavy, bushy tails. On cold days, entire families may huddle together in a single nest to keep warm.

ON LAND

Are cats night creatures?

Yes. Cats' favorite prey are mice, which mostly come out at night. When hunting in dim light, cats open their eyes as wide as possible. With pupils at full size, cats can see about six times better than you! Also, cats have a mirrorlike tapetum behind each eye. The tapetum lets the cat see in almost complete darkness.

Yet cats can also be pretty active during the day. As you know, cats enjoy basking in the warm sunshine. In the bright light, they half-close their eyes to cut down the amount of light that enters. With its pupils closed to just narrow slits, a cat sees about as well as you see.

What other senses help cats hunt in the dark?

Hearing, smell, and touch. A cat's large, sensitive ears pick up all sounds, from the lowest rustle to the highest squeal. A cat's sense of smell is so keen that a newborn kitten can find its mother by scent alone.

The cat feels with its paws and with its long, stiff, and very sensitive whiskers, which are attached to nerves in its skin. The nerves send a message to the brain that tells the cat when it brushes against something—even if it can't see, hear, or smell it!

What sounds do cats make?

None, when hunting. Cats are among the quietest of night creatures. When walking on padded feet, or even jumping from a ledge, they don't make a sound. But when cats fight, it's another story. Two cats screeching at each other at night sound like crying babies or screaming people. During mating season, cats also make lots of noise.

Domestic cat

Lions

Impala

Do lions hunt at night like house cats?

Yes. Lions mostly rest by day and hunt by night. Their main prey are zebras, buffaloes, and antelopes—animals that can easily outrun them.

Lions often hunt in groups. They stalk their prey, much like the way cats stalk mice. When they get to within 100 feet (30 m) of their target, they suddenly leap forward. They either grab a victim with their powerful jaws, or slam it to the ground with their paws.

Lions are not the mighty hunters you might think. They only kill about one out of every four animals they stalk, and they seldom hunt for more than three or four hours a night. Then, it's back to resting. Not a bad life!

Why do lions roar?

Mostly to keep in touch with one another. Sometimes just one lion roars; other times several lions join in a chorus. Experts believe each lion's roar tells the others, "I am here!" This helps members of the pride, or group, stay together, and scares away outsiders.

In the wild, the roar usually starts with one or two softer moans. Then comes the full-throated roar, which you can hear up to 3 miles (5 km) away! The sound lasts about 30 seconds before it fades away to a series of hoarse grunts.

Do leopards hunt like lions?

No. Leopards hunt alone. For this reason, leopards usually go after smaller prey, such as baboons, warthogs, wild dogs, and the young of big animals.

A leopard approaches its prey in an almost snakelike crawl, belly close to the ground. When it is within striking distance, the leopard leaps up and pounces, knocking the prey over. Quickly the big cat buries its two long, sharp fangs in the victim's neck and begins to tear it apart.

After eating its fill, the leopard often carries the leftovers up to a tree. There it drapes itself, and the leftovers, over a branch and takes a nice, long rest.

What night animal is like a big mouse with a pouch?

The opossum. Like mice, opossums are nocturnal animals that have pointed noses and sharp teeth. But like a kangaroo, the female opossum has a pouch on its abdomen for carrying its young.

Female opossums give birth to about 5 to 20 tiny babies at one time. Each is hairless, blind, and deaf at birth and is about the size of a lima bean! An entire litter of 14, for example, weighs less than 1 ounce (28 g) and can easily fit in a soupspoon! The newborns live in the pouch, nursing on their mother's milk.

Do opossums need baby-sitters?

No. Even though the opossum mother is out looking for food every night, her young travel with her.

For the first two months or so, she carries them in her pouch. After that, they crawl out of her pouch and hitch rides on her back for several weeks more. By that time, the nearly full-sized opossums are ready to do their own nighttime food gathering!

What do opossums eat?

Small mice, worms, insects, fruits, roots, and nuts. A particular favorite of small, tree-dwelling opossums is the fruit of the persimmon tree. When persimmons are ripe, some opossums spend the whole night in a tree, stuffing themselves with the fruit.

Who are the opossum's enemies?

Owls, coyotes, foxes, dogs, and cats. When threatened, an opossum lies on its side, unmoving, with eyes closed and tongue hanging out. Since it appears to be dead, predators leave the opossum alone. Now you know the origin of the expression "playing possum," which means pretending to be dead or injured when in danger.

Virginia opossums

What night creatures hunt for food in garbage cans?

Raccoons. Those that live in or near cities will eat almost anything. These "masked bandits" have the amazing ability to break into even the most securely locked trash bins with their long-fingered front paws.

  In the wild, raccoons prefer to search near water for frogs, crayfish, and turtles. Those far from water live on berries, nuts, corn, mice, and insects—things not usually found in garbage cans!

Why do raccoons visit the same spots every night?

It's easier than finding new places in the dark. When day breaks, raccoons usually return to the same place to sleep, too. Country raccoons bed down among tree roots or in a hollow tree. If there are no trees, the raccoons sleep in nests they make in high grass. City raccoons make their homes near people's homes—in sheds, drainpipes, or attics.

Raccoons

Are raccoons endangered animals?

Not at all. In fact, raccoons are growing in number because they can live almost anywhere and eat almost anything. Raccoons adapt well to different habitats—wilderness, farm, or city—and to different climates—from icy cold to tropical.

The raccoons' long gray fur with black tips is camouflage that keeps them well hidden from their enemies. Yet, if attacked, these night creatures become strong, dangerous fighters.

What night creatures are famous for their awful smell?

Skunks. When frightened or under attack, a skunk sends out a horrible-smelling spray from its rear-end scent glands. The most familiar skunk has black fur with bright white stripes from its nose to the tip of its fluffy tail. Other skunks are a solid color or have spots.

Skunks live only in North and South America. They hunt at night in wooded areas for insects, mice, eggs, fruit, and the rotting flesh of dead animals.

What happens before a skunk sprays?

It gives a warning. The skunk may stomp its feet on the ground and give a low hiss or growl. Then, it raises its tail and arches its back. Finally, ZAP!, the smelly, oily liquid shoots out from under the skunk's tail.

How far can a skunk spray?

Up to 12 feet (4 m). The smell chokes nearby animals and they flee. Even worse, the odor can last many days—as people who live in the country know only too well. As bad as the smell is, the spray itself is even worse. If it strikes an eye, the spray can cause burning and temporary blindness. Even one whiff can bring on a stomachache!

Which skunk enemy doesn't mind the smell?

The great horned owl. While hunting at night, this owl does not seem to be bothered by a skunk's spray. Down it swoops to grab the skunk, no matter how strong the odor. Either the horned owl doesn't have much sense of smell—or it just holds its breath!

Spotted skunk

Red fox

Giant desert hairy scorpion

Sun spider

Are spiders night creatures?

Some are. Among them are many hunting spiders that chase insects or lie in wait for them, instead of catching them in webs.

All day long, these hunting spiders hide in nests they build out of the silk they spin from special glands in their bodies. When night falls, they leave their nests to search for food. Even though they have eight very small eyes, many of these spiders are nearly blind. To find a victim, they almost have to bump into it!

Do any night spiders live in your house?

Perhaps. The black-and-white parson spider and the grayish mouse spider spend their days in the dark corners of houses or other buildings. At night, they come out to find food. Some evening you might enter a dark room, turn on the light, and see one of these spiders freeze for a second—and then scurry away.

Do spiders have any night relatives?

Yes, scorpions. Many scorpions live in hot lands and avoid daytime activity in the broiling sun. These creatures only venture out at night, when it's much cooler.

In the darkness, scorpions find the spiders and insects they eat mostly by touch. The scorpion stings its prey with the curved stinger at the end of its tail. One shot of the stinger's poison paralyzes the victim and lets the scorpion enjoy its meal in peace!

But even scorpions are not safe from attack. A fight between a camel spider and a scorpion can end badly for the scorpion. The camel spider prances and sways like a boxer to avoid the scorpion's sting. Then it leaps in and holds onto the scorpion's tail until the spider can bite off the stinger.

Do snakes hunt by sight and sound?

No. Many snakes have very poor eyesight and hearing. Their eyes are best for noticing things that move, not for seeing details. Except for objects close to them, everything looks blurry to a snake. And snakes have no earholes. They pick up sound vibrations from the ground.

How do snakes find their prey in the dark?

Partly by body heat. Many snakes, such as the rattlesnake, have heat-sensitive organs located in deep hollows, or pits, between their nose and eyes. The pits allow these kinds of snakes to detect anything that is even a little warmer than the air.

The sidewinder snake is also well equipped with acute heat sensors. Scientists believe that a sidewinder can follow mice and lizards—sometimes right into their burrows— just by sensing the heat of their bodies.

Why does a snake flick out its tongue?

To pick up smells and taste particles in the air. A snake learns the most about its surroundings with its tongue. A snake's tongue helps it track and catch the animals it eats.

Do snakes bite with their tongues?

No. Snakes bite with special teeth called fangs. Poisonous snakes produce poison in glands near their mouths, and tubes carry the poison from the glands to the fangs.

Sidewinder

Granite night lizard

Snowy
tree crickets

Slugs

Earthworms

Are slugs and worms nocturnal creatures?

Yes. These soft-bodied animals need to keep their bodies moist, which means they must stay out of the sun. When night falls, they creep out of their hiding places to search for food. Sometimes, with a flashlight, you can find them in the garden on a warm, damp night. If you're very quiet, you may even hear their faint rustling in dead leaves.

Which night insect has been around longest?

The cockroach. Fossils of cockroaches date back about 250 million years—to the time of the dinosaurs!

The common cockroach makes its home in food markets, bakeries, restaurants, and people's homes. It belongs to a large family of cockroaches that avoid light and are most active in the dark. Only about ½ inch (1.3 cm) long and a dull tan in color, the common cockroach is not a fussy eater. Food scraps, paper, plants, clothing, dead insects, and just about anything else can make a meal for a cockroach.

Which are the noisiest night creatures?

Tree crickets. Huge numbers gather on trees after dark on warm nights. They produce their loud chirping by rubbing one wing against the other at a rate of about 40 times a second.

Male crickets chirp most. Experts believe it is how they find their mates. Crickets hear with two small spots, or ears, just under the knees of their front legs.

A cricket's chirp changes as the air temperature changes. The higher the temperature, the faster the chirps. On a summer night, count the number of chirps you hear in 15 seconds. Add 40 to that number. The sum will give you the temperature in degrees Fahrenheit.

Are frogs night creatures?

Mostly, even though you can see them during the day. Frogs must stay out of the sun, which dries their skin. Like other amphibians, frogs live in water and on land, and breathe with their lungs. But they also take in oxygen through their thin skin. If their skin is not moist, they can't breathe—and they suffocate.

Are all frogs noisy at night?

No, just the males. Both male and female frogs have vocal cords in their throats, just as we do. But in most species, only the males produce the sounds. They do this by pumping air over their vocal cords. To make the sounds louder, the frogs puff up their throats like balloons. They use these calls to attract females. On summer nights you can hear a bullfrog's booming "jug-o-rums" and "br-wums" from up to 1 mile (1.6 km) away.

Where are frogs during the day?

Some are hiding. These frogs keep cool and damp under rotting tree stumps, piles of leaves, mounds of mud, and around wells, docks, or bridges.

Many tree frogs live in tropical rain forests. They hide during the daylight hours by hanging on to the underside of large tree leaves.

Do frogs ever hide at night?

Yes, when the moon is shining brightly. Frogs keep out of sight so their enemies— snakes, raccoons, and skunks—cannot spot them.

Bullfrogs

Can frogs see well at night?

Yes—especially anything that moves. Good eyesight helps frogs capture food and avoid enemies. Frogs' eyes bulge out from their heads. Each eye is like a tiny periscope on a submarine. The bulging eyes let frogs see in all directions—except directly under their noses. In one experiment, scientists placed food right underneath a frog's head. The frog smelled the food, but had to back away to see it.

How do most frogs hunt?

They sit and wait. As soon as a frog sees a moving bug, fish, or small animal, the frog flips out its sticky tongue. SNAP! In a flash, it snags its prey.

A frog will catch and eat almost anything within reach—as long as it is living. Put a hungry frog near a pile of dead, unmoving flies, and the frog would sooner starve than eat them.

When there is no food aboveground, frogs band together and stir up the mud at the bottom of their pond. This helps them find any tiny creatures that might be hiding there. Really desperate frogs will eat anything, anytime—even one another.

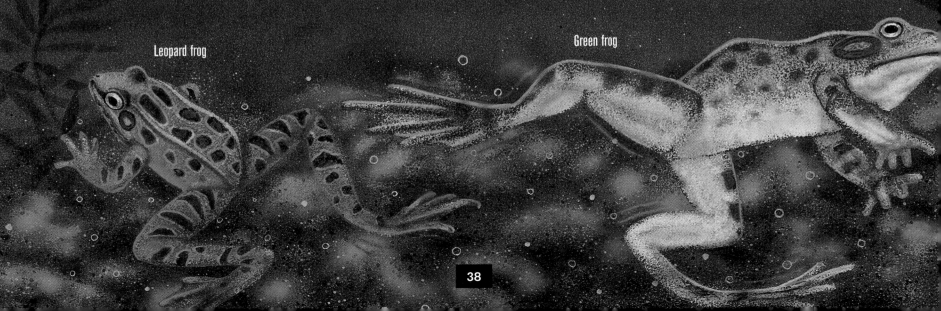

Leopard frog

Green frog

How do frogs swallow their food?

With their eyes! After a frog catches a fly or other prey in its mouth, it blinks. This presses the eyeballs down against the roof of the mouth. The roof bends and pushes the food down into the frog's stomach, all in the blink of an eye!

What happens when a frog eats something poisonous?

It throws up its entire stomach. The stomach hangs out the side of its mouth. Then, using its front legs as wipers, the frog brushes the stomach clean—and swallows it back into its body!

American beavers

Blue gills

Where do beavers live?

In rivers, streams, and lakes. Beavers are active day and night, but they're busiest after dark. That's when they collect the twigs, leaves, bark, and roots that they eat. It's also when beavers use their teeth and front paws to cut down trees and build their houses and dams.

Beavers make their houses, called lodges, of logs, branches, and rocks that they hold together with mud. The lodges look like small islands poking up above the water.

Can beavers breathe underwater?

No. They can hold their breath no longer than about 15 minutes. After that, they must either swim to the surface to take a breath or duck into their lodge, which is filled with air.

Are beavers good swimmers?

Yes, excellent swimmers. Beavers paddle through the water, using their webbed feet as flippers. Scientists have clocked them at speeds of about 5 miles an hour (8 kph). When they swim, beavers steer with their stiff, flat tails. They can also use their tails as an extra paddle when they want to put on a burst of speed.

How does a beaver carry a log through water without choking?

It can shut its throat, even when its mouth is open. In this way the beaver carries logs and branches through the water without swallowing a drop!

How do crocodiles spend the day?

Relaxing. Crocodiles usually spend mornings basking in the warm sunlight of the tropical areas where they live. At midday, when it gets very hot, they seek out a cool, shady spot and rest there for a while. After that, it's back to loafing in the sunshine until the sun sets.

American crocodiles

What do crocodiles do after dark?

They look for food. Some stay in shallow ponds or slow-flowing rivers and wait for prey that come to the water for a drink. Others hide in marshes and swamps, ready to attack any animal that wanders by.

A crocodile can gulp down a small animal, such as a turtle, without chewing. But when it catches a big animal, such as a pig, the crocodile rips out hunks of flesh by snapping its jaws shut and flinging its head from side to side.

Are alligators the same as crocodiles?

Not exactly. Alligators have rounded snouts; crocodile snouts are more pointy. Alligators are slower-moving than crocodiles. Also, the alligator's lower fourth tooth is hidden inside its jaw; the crocodile's lower fourth tooth is on the outside of its jaw.

Are turtles night creatures?

No. But one kind, sea turtles, lay their eggs only at night, and for a very good reason: Eggs laid in damp darkness do not dry out as much as eggs laid in the heat of day.

When ready to lay eggs, the large, heavy female sea turtles crawl out of the water. They waddle up on the beach beyond the high-tide mark. With their back flippers, they dig a pit into which they lay 50 to 100 eggs. Finally, they brush back the sand to completely cover the hole. It's usually dawn before they're done and ready to head back to the sea.

When do sea turtle eggs hatch?

Any time of the day or night. But once they hatch, the baby turtles stay hidden in the sand. They wait until it grows dark and the temperature drops. Only then do the baby turtles climb out of their hiding places and crawl as fast as they can to the water. By waiting until dark, the baby turtles avoid the sun and escape gulls and other daytime predators along the shore.

Which night feeders catch baby sea turtles?

Ghost crabs. All day long these crabs hide under seaweed, stones, or in burrows in the sand. But after sunset, they crawl out to look for food.

The ghost crab's eyes are at the end of two long stalks, which it waves around to spot danger. If a crab sees anything menacing, it scurries back into its burrow. Otherwise, it runs sideways along the sand, picking through seaweed and feeding on sand fleas, dead fish, and, of course, newly hatched sea turtles.

Green sea turtles

Ghost crab

Which shark feeds mostly at night?

The hammerhead. Some scientists have traced the daily activities of a group of hammerheads. By day, the sharks swim in circles around underwater mountains, called seamounts. At dusk, the sharks head for their feeding ground, a distance of about 10 to 15 miles (16 to 24 km). All night long, these sharks gulp down tremendous numbers of squid and different kinds of fish.

   At dawn, the hammerheads make their way back to the seamounts. Strangely enough, they follow the exact same route going and coming.

What other fish feed mostly at night?

Big, fast-swimming fish, such as tuna, swordfish, and marlin. At night, they come up from the deep water to feed on shrimp and smaller fish that live near the surface. The large fish streak through the upper waters, filling their stomachs with the tasty morsels. Then, at dawn, they descend to the lower depths where they stay until it gets dark again. Sometimes the "commute" from deep water to the surface is hundreds of yards (meters) long.

What kinds of animals are night creatures?

Every kind you can think of—mammals, insects, amphibians, reptiles, birds, and fish. Each has a good reason to prefer the darkness of night over the light of day.